1   Introduction

EBay and eBay type auctions are an economic phenomena. EBay is fast becoming a major distribution channel in everything from Beanie Babies to Humvees (Lucking-Reiley (2000); Cohen (2002)).[1] EBay has also become a rich source of data for economists, other social scientists and even computer scientists (Bajari and Hortacsu (2004); Resnick et al. (2003); Zhang et al. (2002)). While eBay may have been built on collectibles, mass produced items have become eBay's best sellers (Cohen (2002)). For example cars are eBay's most important item with $6.7B in annual sales reported in Q3 2003, followed by computers at $2.1B and consumer electronics at $1.9B (Zeithammer (2004a)). In order to use data from eBay or eBay type auctions to estimate the demand for cars, MP3 players or computer monitors, it is necessary to identify the distribution from which each bidder's value for the item is drawn. This paper presents non-parametric identification results for second price open call auctions with private values and unobserved participation. These results cover homogenous auctions, auctions with heterogenous bidders, auctions with observed heterogeneity, auctions with unobserved heterogeneity, and auctions with bidders facing a sequence auctions. It is shown that the traditional demand estimation model (Berry et al. (1995)) is identified given such data. The proof of the result suggest a non-parametric estimator in the tradition of Guerre et al. (2000).

The first section presents two new results for homogenous auctions based on Athey and Haile (2002) and Song (2003). Unless otherwise stated the paper follows Song (2003) and assumes homogenous private value auctions in which bidders are observed at a Bayesian Nash equilibrium.[2] The first result states if the number of potential bidders has a particular functional form, then the value distribution is non-parameterically identified. The second result states that if all bidders bid at their "last opportunity" to do so (unless they are censored) and the timing of "last opportunities" is independently

---

[1] My colleague, Laura Hosken, even bought her wedding dress on eBay!

[2] See Bajari and Hortacsu (2003) for analysis of common value eBay auctions. Such auctions are probably a better description of collectible auctions.

and identically distributed then the value distribution is identified. While the first result is based on a fairly restrictive assumption, it gives a simple function that is straight forward to estimate. The second result shows that this assumption on the distribution of potential number of bidders is not necessary for identification. The second section presents results that generalize the first result to auctions with heterogenous bidders and heterogenous auctions (both observed and unobserved). The third section of the paper presents assumptions and identification results for auctions in which the bidding is interdependent.

The results presented in the first section build on results in Athey and Haile (2002) and Song (2003). Athey and Haile (2002) show that in open call second price auctions with independent private values and a known number of bidders, the value distribution is identified from the observation of one order statistic. For example in second price auctions the price is the $N - 1 : N$ order statistic. That is, the price is all that is needed to identify the value distribution.[3] While this result shows that the value distribution can be identified despite bids being censored, it does not account for the possibility that the existence of the bidder may also be censored. Song (2003) presents a solution to this second censoring problem. Her result is that the value distribution can be identified from the observation of two order statistics. This result works well in the case where the $N : N$ and $N - 1 : N$ order statistics are observed as is the case if eBay provides the data (Adams and Bivins (2004); Zeithammer (2004a)). However, it is unusual to observe the actual highest bids from eBay data and other bidders may have their highest bid censored. Song (2003) presents an identification result for this case, however the estimator based on this result is biased.

This paper follows the structural assumptions of Song (2003) and presents two alternative identification results for the case where the existence of bidders is censored. Estimators based on either result will be unbiased, however the assumptions are more stringent than those presented in Song (2003). The first section present Monte Carlo estimates to compare the different ap-

---

[3]See Rezende (2002) for a straight forward estimation procedure for this case.

proaches. The section's second result uses information on the timing of bids to identify demand. Zhang et al. (2002) assume that a Poisson distribution determines the entry probability and the timing of bids. There are two concerns with their approach. First, it is fairly obvious looking at bidding behavior on eBay that bids are congested towards the end of the auction (Adams et al. (2004)), which suggests the Poisson distribution is not a reasonable representation of bidding behavior. Second, the authors assume that each bidder only bids once at their "last opportunity" which casual observation also suggests is not true.[4] The results presented below indicate that an estimator with less restrictive assumptions can be used to estimate the demand for items on eBay.

The second section of the paper presents results for heterogenous auctions. Athey and Haile (2002) present results for "asymmetric" auctions, that is auctions in which bidders draw their values from different distributions. Again, however, these results are for auctions in which the number of bidders is known. This paper presents results for asymmetric auctions where the number of bidders is unknown.[5] The section also presents results for auctions of differentiated goods. The paper shows that the joint value distribution over multiple items can be identified under certain conditions. The paper further shows that hedonic models are identified and provides assumptions sufficient to identify hedonic models with unobserved item heterogeneity. Bajari and Bankard (2004) presents non-parametric identification results for transactions data with unobserved characteristics. The final result of the section considers auctions with unobserved heterogeneity. Krasnokutskaya (2003) presents identification results for first price auctions and discusses other work on this issue. Athey and Haile (2002) present results for second price auctions with a known number of bidders. Froeb et al. (2001) present a parametric estimator for second price auctions with a common unobserved shock.

---

[4]A Poisson assumption on entry and a non-parametric assumption on the "last opportunity" may be more reasonable. Song has preliminary work on such an estimator.

[5]Froeb et al. (2001) show that power-related parametric distributions can be used to estimate value distributions for asymmetric bidders.

The third section of the paper considers the issue that bidders may shave their bids to account for the option value of winning a future auction. There is a substantial literature on bidding behavior in sequential auctions.[6] However, there is an important difference between traditional sequential auctions and eBay auctions. In a traditional sequential auction such as an FCC spectrum auction, winning bidders leave the sequence of auctions and are not replaced, so the number of bidders and value distribution of the remaining bidders changes over time. On eBay, however, there is constant entry of new bidders into the sequence of auctions. Two recent papers analyze dynamic bidding behavior on eBay (Arora et al. (2002); Zeithammer (2003)), however both papers assume that the bidder faces a finite set of future auctions. In the finite model, bidders in their final auction bid their value for the item as the option value is 0, while bidders in earlier auctions shave their bids to account for the option value of a future auction.[7] This paper assumes that bidders face a infinite set of future auctions. In this context, the paper presents a set of alternative assumptions sufficient to identify the distribution of bidder valuations that is *independent* of the option value of winning a future auction. It is shown that the problem can be represented as a dynamic decision making problem under uncertainty. The argument is similar to the argument presented in Jofre-Bonet and Pesendorfer (2003) although identification comes from assumptions on the savings behavior of the bidders and interest rate regimes.

The paper proceeds as follows. Section 2 presents the model and identification results for the single homogenous auction case. The section also presents a Monte Carlo comparison between the model presented below and the model presented in Song (2003). Section 3 presents identification results that generalize the results in Section 2 to cases where the auctions are heterogenous. Section 4 presents the model and identification results for the infinite sequence of auctions case. Section 5 concludes.

---

[6]See Arora et al. (2002) or Deltas (1999) for a discussion of this literature.

[7]Zeithammer (2004b) presents a model in which bidders strategically account for the effect that there bids have on future auctions. Assumptions used in this paper will rule out this possibility.

2 Homogenous Auction Model

This section presents two identification results. First, it is shown that for a given distribution over the number of potential bidders, the value distribution is identified. The second result is an alternative to the first, showing that the value distribution can be identified with additional assumptions on the distribution of the timing of bids and on the equilibrium bidding behavior.

2.1 The Model and Notation

The model and notation closely follow Song (2003). It is a single eBay auction for a single item. There are N "potential" bidders in the auction, with $p_n = \Pr(N = n)$, and M observed bidders. As stated above this model is of a symmetric private information auction (Assumption 1), where each bidder knows the probability distribution over the number of bidders in the auction (Assumption 2). Assumption 3 is made for simplicity.[8]

Assumption 1 *Each potential bidder's valuation V^i is an independent draw from $F(.)$, where $V^i \in [\underline{v}, \bar{v}]$.*

Assumption 2 *Each potential bidder knows p_n, $F(.)$ and their own value V^i.*

Assumption 3 *There is no minimum bid and there is no minimum increment.*

Finally, the auction lasts for the interval of time $[0, \tau]$ and each bidder is assumed to have a "last opportunity" to bid, although they don't have to bid at that "last opportunity" (Assumption 4).

Assumption 4 *Each potential bidder i is assumed to have a "last opportunity" to bid, $t^i \in [0, \tau]$, which is a random variable, such that the distribution of t^i is denoted $G^i(.)$.*

---

[8]Adams et al. (2004) presents the formula for the case where there is an observable minimum bid.

Let C_t be the "cut off" price at time t. As eBay is a second price auction, $C_t = B_t^{(M-1:M)}$, where $B_t^{(M-1:M)}$ is the second highest bid as of time t. Song (2003) shows that in a Bayesian Nash equilibrium of this game, it must be that for every bidder whose value for the item is greater than C_t at their last opportunity to bid, will bid their value ($B_{ti}^i = V^i$), if they have not already done so.

In each auction, I assume that the amount of the lowest of the two highest bids, $B_\tau^{(M-1:M)}$ or the price, is observed. Note that from above, the price in an eBay auction equals the value of the *potential* bidder with the second highest value. I will denote this value V_2. For the second result of the section I also require that both the number of observed bidders (M) is observed as well as the time of the *latest* of the two highest bids, which is denoted t_2.

In regards to entry into the auction, that decision is endogenous in that only bidders with a positive expected value of entering will enter the auction. This doesn't really mean anything as the cost of entry for each bidder is either assumed to be 0 or infinity and is exogenously determined.[9] So the probability distribution over the number of potential bidders (p_n) is determined exogenously. This assumption contrasts to the entry assumption in Bajari and Hortacsu (2003), who use endogenous entry and a zero-profit condition as part of their identification strategy.

2.2 Results

The following assumption is critical to the main result presented in this section. The distribution allows for any number of bidders in the auction but it places most of the weight on the least number of bidders. The number of bidders is also allowed to vary with the length of the auction.[10] The assumption is used because it allows the probability distribution over the

---

[9]Think of a bidder logging on to eBay at a particular date and time and either having an auction in which to bid (cost of entry is 0) or not having such an auction (cost of entry is infinity).

[10]EBay auctions can last for 3, 5, 7 or 10 days.

price to have a simple functional form.[11]

Assumption 5 *Let $Pr(N = n) = (1 - \tau_j p)\tau_j^n p^n$, where τ_j is the length of auction j, $t_j \in [\underline{\tau}, \bar{\tau}]$ and $p \in (0, \frac{1}{\bar{\tau}})$.*

Given this assumption the following proposition presents the main result of this section of the paper.

Proposition 1 *Given Assumptions (1 - 4) and Assumption 5, if the distribution of $\{V_2\}$ and the length of the auctions are observed, and there is at least two different auction lengths, then $F(.)$ is identified.*

Proof. The proof has three steps. Step 1. Given N, the probability of observing V_2 is

$$\Pr(V_2|N = n) = \frac{n! f(V_2)(1 - F(V_2))F^{n-2}(V_2)}{(n - 2)!} \tag{1}$$

which is the probability that V_2 occurs times the probability that it is the 2nd highest bid. By Assumption 5, $\Pr(N = n) = (1 - \tau_j p)\tau_j^n p^n$. Therefore[12]

$$
\begin{aligned}
\Pr(V_2|N \geq 2, \tau_j) &= (1 - \tau_j p)f(V_2)(1 - F(V_2))(2 + 6\tau_j p F(V_2) + 12\tau_j^2 p^2 F^2(V_2) + \\
&\quad ... + n(n-1)\tau_j^{n-2}p^{n-2}F^{n-2}(V_2) + ...) \\
&= (1 - \tau_j p)f(V_2)(1 - F(V_2))(\sum_{n=2}^{\infty} n(n-1)\tau_j^{n-2}p^{n-2}F^{n-2}(V_2)) \\
&= \frac{2(1-\tau_j p)f(V_2)(1-F(V_2))}{(1-\tau_j p F(V_2))^3}
\end{aligned}
\tag{2}
$$

Step 2. Let $[\underline{v}, \bar{v}]$ be segmented in to K equal disjoint sets such that the union is equal to the original set. Let $v_k = \underline{v} + \frac{k-1}{K}(\bar{v} - \underline{v})$ and

$$f_K(v_k) = \int_{v=v_k}^{v_{k+1}} f(v)dv = F(v_{k+1}) - F(v_k) \tag{3}$$

and

$$F_K(v_k) = \sum_{h=1}^{k-1} f_K(v_h) \tag{4}$$

---

[11]Adams et al. (2004) shows that distribution of *observed* number of bidders for new digital camera auctions on eBay is consistent with this assumption.

[12]Thanks to Joel Schrag for pointing out some of these steps.

Define V_{2k} similarly, such that $V_{2k} \in \{v_1, v_2, ..., v_K\}$. Note that $v_1 = \underline{v}$. Note further that as $K \to \infty$, $F_K(.) \to F(.)$. Let x_k denote the observed (large sample) probability of V_{2k}. So rewriting Equation (2) for the case of V_{2k} and noting that the marginal probability of observing v_k is $f_k(v_k)$ and the cumulative probability of observing v_k is $F_K(v_k)$ we have the following equation.

$$x_k = \frac{2(1 - \tau_j p) f_K(V_{2k})(1 - F_K(V_{2k}))}{(1 - \tau_j p F_K(V_{2k}))^3} \tag{5}$$

Step 3. First we have

$$x_1 = 2(1 - \tau_j p) f_K(\underline{v}) \tag{6}$$

So consider two sets of auctions with different lengths, τ_1 and τ_2, we have

$$x_{11} = 2(1 - \tau_1 p) f_K(\underline{v}) \tag{7}$$

and

$$x_{12} = 2(1 - \tau_2 p) f_K(\underline{v}) \tag{8}$$

Rearranging we have

$$\frac{x_{11}}{2(1 - \tau_1 p)} = \frac{x_{12}}{2(1 - \tau_2 p)} \tag{9}$$

and so

$$p = \frac{x_{12} - x_{11}}{\tau_1 x_{12} - \tau_2 x_{11}} \tag{10}$$

and

$$f_K(\underline{v}) = \frac{x_{11}}{2(1 - \tau_1 p)} \tag{11}$$

and rearranging Equation (5)

$$f_K(V_{2k}) = \frac{2(1 - \tau_j p) x_k (1 - F_K(V_{2k}))}{(1 - \tau_j p F_K(V_{2k}))^3} \tag{12}$$

Using Equation 4, by induction $f_K(.)$ is identified. Letting $K \to \infty$, $F(.)$ is identified. Q.E.D.

Proposition 1 states that if the potential number of bidders has a particular functional form, the distribution of prices and two different auction lengths are observed, then the value distribution is identified. The proof shows that given a particular probability distribution over the number of potential bidders the value distribution unconditional on the number of bidders is also identified and has a relatively simple functional form.

$$\Pr(V_2|N \geq 2, \tau_j) = \frac{2(1 - \tau_j p)f(V_2)(1 - F(V_2))}{(1 - \tau_j p F(V_2))^3} \tag{13}$$

As one would expect the functional form is a slightly more complicated version of the standard censoring model. If one is willing to assume that a log normal distribution is parsimonious representation of the underlying distribution then the formula suggests a simple maximum likelihood estimator (Greene (2000)). Alternatively, the three steps of the proof suggest a non-parametric estimator in the tradition of Guerre et al. (2000).

The second result of this section shows that there is a third way to identify demand from eBay auctions, and that this third way doesn't rely on some arbitrary distributional assumption. However, additional assumptions are still used to prove the result. In particular, the following assumption states that every bidder's last opportunity to bid is independently and identically distributed.

Assumption 6 *Let $G^i(.) = G(.)$ for all i.*

Assumption 7 *If given the opportunity to do so, all bidders make a bid at their "last opportunity" to do so.*

Assumption 7 states that we are going to restrict the set of BNEs to those in which all bidders bid at their last opportunity to do so, if they have that opportunity. Song (2003) shows that such equilibria exists although this is a more restrictive structural assumption than what is presented in Song (2003). As discussed above, there is a very large tendency for eBay bidders to bid at the end of the auction (see Adams et al. (2004) for example), and so I don't believe it is an overly restrictive assumption. Below, I present a lemma which suggests that bidders will always bid late in equilibrium (Lemma 2).

Proposition 2 *Given that Assumptions (1 - 4) and Assumptions 6 and 7 hold, and $\{M\}$, the timing of the highest and second highest bids, the auction length and $\{V_2\}$ are observed, then $F(.)$ is identified.*

Proof. Step 1. As neither the second highest nor the highest bidder is censored, by Assumption 7 we observe the distribution of the timing of bids for the second highest and the highest bidder. By Assumption 6 we observe $G(.)$. Step 2. Let t_2 denote the latest of the bids from the two highest bidders. We can write the probability that there will be two bidders and a particular set of bids and timing of bids in the following manner.

$$\Pr(M = 2, t_2, V_2 | N \geq 2) = 2g(t_2)G(t_2)f(V_2)(1 - F(V_2))$$
$$\times \left(\sum_{n=2}^{\infty} p_n(n - 1)nF^{n-2}(V_2)(1 - G(t_2))^{n-2}\right) \tag{14}$$

Note that p_n is undefined and is just $\Pr(N = n)$. We know that $G(\tau) = 1$, so[13]

$$\Pr(M = 2, \tau, V_2 | N \geq 2) = 4p_2 g(\tau)f(V_2)(1 - F(V_2)) \tag{15}$$

Note that $g(\tau)$ is observed from Step (1). Following similar reasoning to the proof of Proposition 1, we create K equal and disjoint sets such that the union of the sets is equal to $[\underline{v}, \bar{v}]$ and define f_K and F_K. Noting that $F(\underline{v}) = 0$ from Equation 15 we have

$$x_1 = 4g(\tau)p_2 f_K(\underline{v}) = 4g(\tau)p_2 f_K(V_{21}) \tag{16}$$

where x_1 is observed and we can solve for $p_2 f_K(V_{21})$. Second we have

$$p_2 f_K(V_{2k}) = \frac{x_k}{4g(\tau)(1 - F_K(V_{2k}))} \tag{17}$$

and

$$F_K(V_{2k}) = \sum_{h=1}^{k-1} f_K(V_{2h}) \tag{18}$$

By induction we can solve for $p_2 f_K(V_{2k})$ as a function of observables for all k. As the marginal probabilities must some to 1,

$$\sum_{k=1}^{K} p_2 f_K(V_{2k}) = p_2 \sum_{k=1}^{K} f_K(V_{2k}) = p_2 \tag{19}$$

---

[13]I am assuming that this is true as $t_2 \to \tau$, or that $0^0 = 1$.

Letting $K \to \infty$ we have the result. Q.E.D.

Proposition 2 provides a third identification result for auctions in which the number of potential bidders is unknown. Unlike Proposition 1 the result here is not based on some relatively arbitrary functional form assumption. Rather it is based on the assumption that the timing of bids is independently and identically distributed and on structural assumption that in equilibrium all bidders bid at their last opportunity if their valuation is above the cutoff price at their last opportunity. While this structural assumption is more restrictive than the structural assumptions presented in Song (2003) there is an observed tendency for bidders to bid late in eBay auctions as well as some theoretical justification (see Lemma 2).

The next section compares a version of the estimator based on Proposition 1 with a version of the estimator presented in Song (2003).

2.3 Monte Carlo

This section undertakes a Monte Carlo comparison between the estimator presented in Proposition 1 and the estimator presented in Song (2003). For simplicity it is assumed that f is *known* to be normally distributed $N(\mu, \sigma^2)$.[14] The auctions are generated assuming two different distributions over the number of potential bidders. First, it is assumed that $\Pr(N = n) = (1 - \tau_j p)\tau_j^n p^n$ (Assumption 5) where $p = 0.9$ and $\tau_j = 1$. Second, I assume Bernoulli distribution of entry (N is distributed Binomial with 100 trials and p probability of success) where $p = .02$. Finally, an exponential distribution with $\lambda = 2$ is assumed for the timing of the bids ($G(.)$).

The Song model is a simplified version of the model presented in Song (2003) and the Adams model is a simplified version of the model presented in Proposition 1. Note that for the Song model auctions with fewer than

---

[14]That is, the simulations just estimate μ, σ and p. Song (2003) presents Monte Carlo results for her semi-parametric estimator under alternative distributional assumptions on the Monte Carlo data. Note that Adams et al. (2004) presents estimates from both models from actual eBay data.

Assumptions	Variable	Actual	Reps	Mean	SD	Min	Max
Song							
drop if	μ	2.00	1000	2.02	.09	1.59	2.25
$t_2 < .4$	σ	.50	1000	.50	.04	.39	.63
No drop	μ	2.00	1000	2.23	.03	2.12	2.31
	σ	.50	1000	.49	.02	.44	.55
Adams							
	μ	2.00	1000	2.00	.08	1.70	2.21
	σ	.50	1000	.50	.01	.46	.56
	p	.90	1000	.90	.03	.79	.96

Table 1: Monte Carlo Estimates with $p_n = (1-p)p^n$

3 bidders are dropped. This is because Song's approach requires that two order statistics are observed and in most cases this will be the high bids from the second and third highest bidders. Auctions in which the latest of the highest bids of the two highest bidders occurs early in the auction may also be dropped. For Song's model to give an unbiased estimate of the distribution it must be that the bids of the third highest *potential* bidder are observed. However, it may be that the third highest potential bidder has their highest bid or their existence censored. Song shows that this censoring bias is more likely to be a problem the earlier in the auction the two highest bidders bid. Song presents a method for choosing the optimal number of auctions to throw away given the trade off between bias and efficiency. Here the cut off is chosen arbitrarily. For the Adams model, auctions with fewer than 2 bidders are dropped.

Table 1 presents the results assuming that the probability distribution over the number of potential bidders follows Assumption 5. In the case of the Song model, the table presents results with different restrictions on the auctions that are used to do the estimation. The top set of results is based on a restriction that only auctions in which the latest of the two highest bidders bids after 0.4 are used. This restrictions reduces the data

Assumptions	Variable	Actual	Reps	Mean	SD	Min	Max
Song							
drop if	μ	2.00	1000	2.01	.06	1.78	2.18
$t_2 < .4$	σ	.50	1000	.50	.04	.43	.55
No drop	μ	2.00	1000	2.08	.03	2.00	2.16
	σ	.50	1000	.49	.02	.43	.55
Adams							
	μ	2.00	1000	2.00	.07	1.79	2.26
	σ	.50	1000	.47	.01	.45	.50
	p	.02	1000	.59	.10	.03	.81

Table 2: Monte Carlo Estimates with $p_n = (1-p)^{100-n} p^n$

set by between 60% and 80%. The results show that Song's estimator gives a slightly biased estimate of μ, 2.02 rather than 2, however the estimator is relatively inefficient. The second set of results is based results in which no restriction is made about which auctions can be used. We see that in this case the estimator is biased upwards but the estimate of μ is made with a lot more precision. Comparing the results to the estimator based on Proposition 1, the estimates for μ are not biased while being a little more efficient than Song's less biased estimator.

Table 2 presents results from Monte Carlos under a different assumption on the number of potential bidders in each auction. It is assumed that $p_n = .98^{100-n} .02^n$. Note that while this distribution is different from the one presented above, it still places most of its weight on there being a small number of bidders in each auction. The results show that even though the distributional assumption does not hold, the estimator presented above still gives an unbiased estimate for μ. However that estimate is slightly less efficient than the less biased estimator based on Song (2003). Note also that the Adams estimator gives a biased estimate for σ and this estimate is more biased than the two Song estimates for σ. Finally, note that the estimate for p from the Adams model is nonsense, which is not surprising given that the

13

distributional assumption is incorrect.

3 Heterogenous Auctions

This section presents results which generalize Proposition 1 to situations where the auctions heterogenous, including heterogenous bidders (asymmetric auctions), heterogenous items, and unobserved auction heterogeneity.

3.1 Heterogenous Bidders

The next two results generalize the first result to the case where bidders have observable characteristics. The major issue here is that the level of observation is an auction, not a bidder. Thus it is necessary to infer information about the population of bidders from observing just the identities of the winning and second highest bidders.

Assumption 8 *Let V_A^i be distributed $F_A(.)$ for all bidders such that i has observable characteristic A. Let V_B^j be distributed $F_B(.)$ for all bidders such that j has observable characteristic B.*

Assumption 8 states that bidders can be one of two types and conditional on their type their valuations are independently and identically distributed. The following proposition states that the identification result presented above can be generalized to this case.

Proposition 3 *If Assumptions (1 - 4) and Assumptions 5 and 8 hold, then if the distribution of $\{V_2\}$, the identity of the highest bidder and the second highest bidder and the length of the auctions are observed, and there are at least two different auction lengths, $F_A(.)$ and $F_B(.)$ are identified.*

Proof. By Assumption 8 we have $F(v) = qF_A(v) + (1 - q)F_B(v)$ where q is the unconditional probability that bidder i has characteristic A. By

Assumption 5, from Proposition 1, $F(v)$ is identified from the observation of $\{V_2\}$. Therefore, rewriting Equation (13) for this case

$$Pr(V_2, 1 \in A, 2 \in B | N \geq 2, \tau_j) = x_1 = \frac{2(1 - \tau_j p)(1 - q) f_B(V_2) q(1 - F_A(V_2))}{(1 - \tau_j p F(V_2))^3}$$

(20)

where the highest bidder is of type A and the second highest bidder is of type B. Let

$$Pr(V_2, 1 \in A, 2 \in A | N \geq 2, \tau_j) = x_2 = \frac{2(1 - \tau_j p) q f_A(V_2) q(1 - F_A(V_2))}{(1 - \tau_j p F(V_2))^3}$$

(21)

Therefore

$$\frac{x_1}{x_2} = \frac{(1 - q)(f_B(V_2))}{q f_A(V_2)}$$

(22)

Substituting in $f(V_2)$ and solving for $q f_A(V_2)$

$$q f_A(V_2) = \frac{x_2 f(V_2)}{x_1 + x_2}$$

(23)

By adding up we have

$$\int_{\underline{v}}^{\bar{v}} q f_A(v) dv = q$$

(24)

Q.E.D.

Proposition 3 states that if bidder i is of one of two types, those types are observable, and conditional on type the value distribution is independently and identically distributed, then the value distribution conditional on type is identified. The result follows in straight forward manner from Proposition 1. As the bidder's type is observed, the unconditional probability that a particular price is observed is a function of the unconditional probability that the bidder is of a particular type and the value distribution given the bidder's type. This result is useful if the data allows the econometrician to observe bidder characteristics such as zip code, reputation score or bids in previous auctions. The following corollary generalizes this proposition.

Assumption 9 *Let bidder i have observable characteristic $A \in \mathcal{A}$, then V_A^i is independently and identically distributed $F_A(.)$.*

15

Assumption 9 states that the observable characteristics could have any general form. That is, it could be a dummy variable like gender or continuous variable like income.

Corollary 1 *If Assumptions (1 - 4) and Assumption 5 and 9 hold, then if the distribution of $\{V_2\}$, the length of the auctions and the identity of the bidders are observed, and there at least two different auction lengths, then $F_A(.)$ is identified for all $A \in \mathcal{A}$.*

Proof. The proof has four steps. Step 1. Let $\mathcal{A}$ be split into K equal and disjoint sets such that $\bigcup_{k=1}^{K} A_k = \mathcal{A}$, and the unconditional probability that bidder i has characteristic A_k is q_k. Now consider two sets A_1 and its complement. By Proposition 3, F_{A_1} and q_1 are identified. Step 2. Consider the union of A_1 and A_2, denoted A_{12} and its complement. Again from Proposition 3, $F_{A_{12}}$ and $q_1 + q_2$ are identified. So from Step (1) q_2 is identified and as $F_{A_{12}} = q_1 F_{A_1} + q_2 F_{A_2}$, F_{A_2} is identified. Step 3. By induction F_{A_k} and q_k are identified for all $k \in \{1, 2, ..., K\}$. Step 4. Let $K \to \infty$ and we have that $F_A(.)$ is identified for all $A \in \mathcal{A}$. Q.E.D.

Corollary 1 states that if the bidder has an observable characteristic and that characteristic has a general form, i.e. is either discrete or continuous, then the value distribution conditional on the observable characteristics is identified. The result follows in straight forward manner from Proposition 3. Again, this result is useful if the auction data also includes other information about the bidder.

3.2   Heterogenous Items

The result presented in this section generalizes the first result to the case where we observe bidding across auctions for heterogenous items. The first result shows that when the number of items is small it is possible to identify the joint value distribution. The last three results show that a model in the tradition of Berry et al. (1995) can be identified. That is, items can be mapped into characteristic space with an unobserved item characteristic and the function is allowed to vary with observed characteristics of the bidders.

Consider *two* simultaneous auctions, one for item A and the second for item B. Previous results show that under certain assumptions it is possible to identify $F_j(.)$ where $j \in \{A, B\}$. The following corollary states that it is possible to identify the joint value distribution, $F(., .)$.

Assumption 10 *Let* $Pr(N_j = n) = (1 - \tau_{jk}p_j)\tau_{jk}^n p_j^n$, *where* $j \in \{A, B\}$ *and* $p_j \in (0, \frac{1}{\tau})$.

Assumption 10 generalizes Assumption 5 to this case. Note that bidders may bid in both auctions without restriction but they don't have to. The following assumption is made for simplicity.[15]

Assumption 11 *Let bidder* i's *bids across auctions be independent.*

Corollary 2 *Given Assumptions (1 - 4) and Assumptions 10 and 11, if the distribution of* $\{V_{2A}, V_{2B}\}$ *is observed, the length of the auctions for each set of auctions, and one bidder is observed to bid in both auctions such that she has neither the highest or second highest bid in either auction, and there are at least two auction lengths for each set of auctions, then* $F(., .)$ *is identified.*

Proof. Consider *only* the set of auctions in which *one* bidder is observed to bid in both auctions without being the highest or second highest bid in either, then the conditional probability is

$$
\begin{aligned}
x_1 &= (1 - \tau_{Aj}p_A)(1 - \tau_{Bk}p_B)f_A(V_{2A})(1 - F_A(V_{2A}))f_B(V_{2B})(1 - F(V_{2B})) \\
&\quad \times F(V_{2A}, V_{2B})(\sum_{n=3}^{\infty} n(n - 1)\tau_{Aj}^{n-3} p_A^{n-3} F_A^{n-3}(V_{2A}) \\
&\quad \times ((\sum_{n=3}^{\infty} n(n - 1)\tau_{Bk}^{n-3} p_B^{n-3} F_B^{n-3}(V_{2B})))
\end{aligned}
\tag{25}
$$

By Proposition 1, $F_A(.)$, $F_B(.)$, p_A and p_B are identified, so $F(., .)$ is identified. Q.E.D.

---

[15]See the last section for a discussion of the case where bids across auctions are interdependent.

Traditionally the demand for differentiated products is estimated by assuming that product choices can be mapped into observed and unobserved product characteristics and using hedonic regression models (Berry et al. (1995)). The major argument for doing this is that there are often so many different products that it is not possible to identify the demand for each product without using information about the demand for similar products.[16] The following results suggest that a similar model can be used with eBay type data.

Assumption 12 *Let V_j^i be distributed $F(., X_j)$ where X_j is a J dimensional vector of observed item characteristics.*

Assumption 12 states that the value distribution is some general function of the set of observed characteristics of the item X_j. An example would be a random coefficients model (Berry et al. (1995); Nevo (2000)). Note that in Berry et al. (1995) and more recently Bajari and Bankard (2004) there is a unobserved component of the product characteristics, this issue is discussed below. As above, the probability distribution on the number of potential bidders can vary across items.

Assumption 13 *Let $Pr(N_j = n) = (1 - \tau_{jk}p_j)\tau_{jk}^n p_j^n$, for all j items, such that $p_j \in (0, \frac{1}{\tau})$.*

Corollary 3 *If Assumptions (1 - 4) and Assumptions 12 and 13 hold, then if $\{V_2\}$ and X_j are observed for all items j, and the auction length is observed for two different auction lengths for all items j, then $F(., X_j)$ is identified.*

Proof. By Proposition 1, given X_j, $F(.|X_j)$ is identified. Therefore, for all X_j, $F(., X_j)$ is identified. Q.E.D.

Corollary 3 shows that it is straight forward to generalize Proposition 1 to a hedonic model. The rest of the section considers a model with unobserved item heterogeneity.

---

[16]Part of the identification strategy in this literature is to use this variation in product characteristics.

18

Assumption 14 *Let $V_j^i = v_{ij} + \xi_j$ where v_{ij} is distributed $F(., X_j)$ and $\xi_j \in [\underline{\xi}, \bar{\xi}]$, X_j is a J dimensional vector of observable characteristics of the item, and ξ_j is a characteristic of the item observed by the bidder and unobserved by the researcher.*

Note that ξ_j is constant across auctions for the same item. That is it represents some unobserved characteristic about the car or MP3 player rather than some unobserved characteristic that is auction specific. The next section discusses identification when there is unobserved auction heterogeneity. An important simplification in Assumption 14 is that unobserved item heterogeneity enters the value function additively. This assumption makes identification straightforward, but one may be concerned that it is unnecessarily simple (Bajari and Bankard (2004)).

Proposition 4 *If Assumptions (1 - 4) and Assumptions 13 and 14 hold, then if $\{V_2\}$ and X_j are observed for all items j, the auction length for at least two lengths for all items j, then $F(., X_j)$ and ξ_j are identified.*

Proof. Step 1. Let $G(., X_j)$ be the distribution of $v_{ij} + \xi_j$. For a given item j by Corollary 3, $G_j(., X_j)$ is identified. Step 2. Let there be two items j and k such that $X_j = X_k$, then for some $a > b$ such that $G_j(a, X_j) = G_k(b, X_j)$, $a - b = \xi_j - \xi_k$. When this difference is equal to $\bar{\xi} - \underline{\xi}$, $\xi_j = \bar{\xi}$ and $\xi_k = \underline{\xi}$, and so $F(., X_j)$ and ξ_j are identified. Q.E.D.

Proposition 4 shows that Corollary 3 can be generalized to the case of unobserved item heterogeniety. Identification comes from comparing the distributions for items with similar observed characteristics.

The final result shows that the model can be generalized to include observed characteristics of the bidders. In the example of estimating the demand for cars, this may be gained from demographic information obtained from observing the zip codes of individual bidders.

Assumption 15 *Let $V_j^i = v_{ij} + \xi_j$ where v_{ij} is distributed $F(., X_j, Z_i)$ and $\xi_j \in [\underline{\xi}, \bar{\xi}]$, X_j is a J dimensional vector of observable characteristics of the* *item, Z_i is an I dimensional vector of observable characteristics of the bidder and ξ_j is a characteristic of the item observed by the bidder and unobserved by the researcher.*

Proposition 5 shows that a model in the tradition of Berry et al. (1995) can be identified using eBay type auction data.

Proposition 5 *If Assumptions (1 - 4) and Assumptions 13 and 15 hold, then if $\{V_2\}$, X_j, Z_i, the auction lengths are observed for all j and the identity of the highest bidder and the second highest bidder are observed, and there are at least two auctions lengths for all items j, then $F(., X_j, Z_i)$ and ξ_j are identified.*

Proof. Let $G(., X_j, Z_i)$ be the distribution of $v_{ij} + \xi_j$. For a given item j using a similar argument to Corollary 3, $G_j(., X_j, Z_i)$ is identified by Corollary 1. The rest of the proof follows directly from the proof of Proposition 4. Q.E.D.

The proof of Proposition 5 is similar to the proof of Proposition 4 except that in this case the proof generalizes Corollary 1.

A major objective of this paper is to show that eBay type auction data can be used to estimate the demand for differentiated goods and suggest a method for such estimation. Proposition 5 shows that a traditional demand model is identified using such data. Such a model can account for a large number of items with bidder preferences allowed to vary generally with observed item characteristics.

3.3 Unobserved Auction Heterogeneity

This section considers auctions in which individual bidders observe information about the value of the item that is unobserved by the researcher. The main result is a proposition that shows it is possible to identify the value distribution if the researcher observes the same bidders bidding in a large number of auctions. This section presents assumptions and data requirements for identifying demand with both unobserved auction heterogeneity and unobserved number of bidders. The first result states that if the distribution has two mass points an equal distance from 0, then the value distribution is identified if at least one bidder i is observed bidding in two simultaneous auctions. The second result states that as the number of auctions that bidder i is observed to bid in gets large, then for any distribution for the unobserved heterogeneity (Γ), the value distribution is identified.

Assumption 16 *Let $V_j^i = V^i - y_j$, where $y_j \in [\underline{y}, \bar{y}]$ is observed by bidder i and distributed $\Gamma(.)$.*

Assumption 16 states that there is some unobserved heterogeneity that is additive to the value of the item and the same for every bidder in a particular auction. Note that in this section j refers to the auction rather than the item. The following assumption states that the distribution of the unobserved heterogeneity has a simple symmetric two mass point distribution.

Assumption 17 *Let $\Gamma(.)$ be such that $y \in \{-a, a\}$ where $\Pr(y = a) = \gamma$ and $a > 0$ and $\gamma \in (0, 1)$*

This assumption and the assumption (below) that the researcher observes at least one bidder bid in two simultaneous auctions, is enough to identify the value distribution. The assumption that the two auctions are simultaneous and the bid in each auction is independent of the bid in the other auction, is made for simplicity. The next section considers identification issues when bids are not independent.

Assumption 18 *Let each bidder i bid on 2 simultaneous auctions such that her bids across auctions are independent.*

Definition 1 *Let $\mathcal{A}_t$ be the set of auctions such that at least one bidder i is not censored at their last opportunity to bid after t in both auctions and is not the highest bid in the auctions.*

Note that the second highest bidder is never censored. Given these assumptions the following proposition illustrates the basic result of the section.

Proposition 6 *Let Assumptions (1 - 4) and Assumption 5, 16, 17 and 18 hold, then if the distribution of prices $\{B_{21}, B_{22}\}$, the bidder's identities, the auction lengths, and the amount of the bids (other than the winning bid) are observed, and there is more than one auction length, then considering the set of auctions $\mathcal{A}_t$, as $t \to \tau$, $F(.)$ is identified.*

Proof By Assumption 17, there is some subset of $\mathcal{A}_t$ such that $|B_{t1}^i - B_{t2}^i| > 0$. As $t \to \tau$, $|B_{t1}^i - B_{t2}^i| = |V_1^i - V_2^i| = 2a$, and so we observe $\{V_2\}$ as if $V_1^i > V_2^i$, then $B_{21} = V_2 - a$. By Proposition 1, $F(.)$ is identified. Q.E.D.

The proposition states that if the distribution of the unobserved auction heterogeneity is relatively simple and at least one bidder is observed to bid in two auctions then the value distribution can be identified. The result follows from the observation in Song (2003) that bidders who have are not censored at their last opportunity will bid their value for the item. In this case we observe the difference between the two valuations.

The next result shows that it is possible to identify demand under a more general assumption on the distribution of unobserved heterogeneity, however the requirements on the data are correspondingly larger.

Assumption 19 *Let each bidder i bid on J simultaneous auctions such that her bids across auctions are independent.*

Proposition 7 *Let Assumptions (1 - 4) and Assumptions 5, 16 and 19 hold, then if the distribution of prices $\{B_{21}, B_{22}, ..., B_{2J}\}$, the auction lengths, the identities of the bidders and all the bids except the highest are observed, and there is more than one auction length, then as $J \to \infty$ and considering the set of auctions $\mathcal{A}_t$ as $t \to \tau$, $F(.)$ is identified.*

Proof. Step 1. Let the set $[\underline{y}, \bar{y}]$ be split into J equal and disjoint sets of length a_J. Let $y_j = \underline{y} + (j-1)a_J$. Step 2. Let each bidder bid in J auctions. There is a subset of $\mathcal{A}_t$ such that for at least one bidder i the J auctions can be ordered, $|B_{t1}^i > B_{t2}^i > ... > B_{tJ}^i|$. As $t \to \tau$, $|B_{tj}^i - B_{tj+1}^i| = |V_{tj}^i - V_{tj+1}^i| = a_J$, $V^i = B_{tj}^i + \bar{y} - ja_J$ and so $V_2 = B_{21} + \bar{y} - a_J$. As $J \to \infty$, by Proposition 1,

$F(.)$ is identified. Q.E.D.

The proposition states that as the number of auctions in which the research observes a particular individual bidding gets large, the underlying value distribution can be identified even with fairly general assumptions on the distribution of unobserved heterogeneity. The results presented in this section suggest that there is a trade-off between assumptions on the unobserved heterogeneity and the requirements on the data.

4   An Infinite Sequence of Auctions

Another major concern with using bidding on eBay to estimate demand is that bidders may shave their bids in order to account for the option value of winning a future auction. This section models bidding in such an environment and presents assumptions sufficient to identify the underlying value distribution. Knowing the underlying value distribution may be important for policy analysis and merger analysis. The first part considers a bidder facing an infinite sequences of identical auctions while the second part considers the case where the items are similar but differentiated but the bidder is still only looking to buy one item from the sequence of auctions.

When bidding for a single item sold in a sequence of auctions, the cost of winning a particular auction at time t includes both the opportunity cost of the money and the cost of giving up the opportunity of winning the item in some future auction. The "right" to bid in a future auction can be thought of as an option. If a bidder only wants one item then by winning the auction she gives up this option. Thus when buying a single item in a sequence of auctions the consumer surplus from winning the item in a particular auction (t) is equal to the value of the item V^i less the price paid for the item, $B_t^{(M-1:M)}$, less the value of the option (the opportunity cost of winning) (Dixit and Pindyck (1994)). The value of this option is denoted O_t^i and below it is shown to be a function of the bidder's time preference, δ_i, the value of the item (V^i), the probability of winning a particular future auction ($\Pr(B_{t+s}^i > B_{t+s}^{(M-1:M)})$)

23

the expected price conditional on winning ($E(B_{t+s}^{(M-1:M)}|B_{t+s}^i > B_{t+s}^{(M-1:M)})$) and the option value of winning that auction (O_{t+s}^i).

4.1 Homogenous Auctions

The following set of assumptions are made in order to simplify the game and turn it into a dynamic decision making problem under uncertainty.[17] Let $\mathcal{A}$ denote the set of all auctions and $\mathcal{I}$ the set of all potential bidders. The following assumption is that each bidder faces a known discrete infinite set of future auctions.

Assumption 20 *Let each bidder i faces at time t a known infinite sequence of auctions, $\mathcal{A}_t^i = \{A_t^i, A_{t+1}^i, A_{t+2}^i, ...\} \subset \mathcal{A}$ where $i \in \mathcal{I}$.*

However, while the particular bidder knows which set of auctions she is bidding on, the only information that she has about her competing bidders is the probability distribution p_{nt}.

Assumption 21 $\mathcal{A}_t^i$ *is known to i but unknown to $j \neq i$.*

Assumptions 21 and 22 are made so that nothing about future competitors is learned from who bids what and who wins what in past auctions. While these assumptions seem somewhat arbitrary the sheer number of auctions and bidders on eBay suggests that it is difficult for bidders to learn about the bids and participation in future auctions from the behavior and outcomes of past auctions.

Assumption 22 *If bidder i wins auction A_t^i then she leaves the sequence, and is replaced by some bidder i_{new} such that V^{inew} is distributed $f(.)$ and $\mathcal{A}_{t+1}^i = \mathcal{A}_{t+1}^{inew}$.*

---

[17]Jofre-Bonet and Pesendorfer (2003) show in a somewhat general setting how dynamic auction games with Markov Perfect equilibria can be turned into a dynamic decision making problem. Zeithammer (2004a) shows that bidders in actual auctions seem to behave as if the problem is a dynamic decision making problem rather than a dynamic game. One explanation is that there is just too much new entry and too many new auctions for the bidder in one auction to have a "pivotal" effect on the outcome of a future auction.

The assumptions contrast to the assumptions made in Zeithammer (2004b). In that paper, bidders know about future auctions and behave strategically by making bids that affect the expected value of winning future auctions. Zeithammer (2004b) calculates the equilibrium of the dynamic game for the 2 period and 3 period case. The simplifying assumption made above turns the problem into a dynamic decision making problem. It is further assumed that these auction do not overlap in time. There may be a concern that some auctions are occurring simultaneously and a bidder may have to choose between them, however this issue is assumed away for simplicity.[18] Each auction, A_t^i, is as presented in the previous section and in Song (2003).

Assumption 23 *Let $p_{tn} = p_n$, $F_t(.) = F(.)$, and $G_t^i(.) = G^i(.)$ for all $t \in \{1, 2, ...\}$.*

Assumption 23 states that the model is stationary. This assumption simplifies the analysis and distinguishes the problem from models analyzed in the literature (Deltas (1999)).

Lemma 1 *Given Assumptions (1 - 4) and Assumptions (20 - 23), in any Bayes Nash equilibrium of the "super" game, $B_t^i = B^i = V^i - O^i$.*

It is straight forward to see that given that nobody learns anything about participation in future auctions from observing bidding and outcomes in past auctions and that the exogenous parameters are all stable over time (Assumption 23), then it must be that in equilibrium $B_t^i = B^i$.[19] It follows from above that the actual value of winning the auction is $V^i - O^i$. It then follows from Song (2003) that in every BNE, $B^i = V^i - O^i$, where B^i is assumed to be the bid of the bidder when the bidder has an opportunity to bid at her last opportunity. Note that I use B^i and $V^i - O^i$ interchangeably.

---

[18]Zeithammer (2004a) shows that even though auctions may end sequentially there is a sense in which they are actually simultaneous. In particular, if the existence of a future auction is revealed prior to the end of the current auction it may be optimal for the bidder not to bid on the current auction. This would occur if the bidder's "net value" for the item, ie their value for the item less their option value, is less than 0.

[19]I'm not assuming Markov Perfect equilibria but just claiming that in every Bayes Nash equilibria of this game the bidding functions are stationary.

Definition 2 *Let $H(.)$ be the distribution of B_t^i which is on the support $[\underline{b}, \bar{b}]$.*

Above and in Song (2003) it is shown that $H(.)$ can be identified from observing the auction prices and certain other data. Let δ_i define bidder i's preferences over time. Given this result and assuming δ_i is constant over time, the option value can be written in the following recursive manner

$$
\begin{aligned}
O^i(B^i) &= \delta_i \Pr(B^i > B^{(M-1:M)}) E(B^i - B^{(M-1:M)} | B^i > B^{(M-1:M)}) \\
&\quad + \delta_i(1 - \Pr(B^i > B^{(M-1:M)})) O^i(B^i)
\end{aligned}
\tag{26}
$$

By winning the auction at time t the bidder gives up the value of the winning the auction at time $t+1$ which is the probability of winning the auction $(\Pr(B^i > B^{(M-1:M)}))$ by the expected value of winning the auction given that the bidder won $(E(B^i - B^{(M-1:M)} | B^i > B^{(M-1:M)}))$. There is also some probability that they lose the next auction in which case their continuation value is equal to the option value. This equation can be rearranged to give

$$
O^i(B^i) = \frac{\delta_i \Pr(B^i > B^{(M-1:M)}) E(B^i - B^{(M-1:M)} | B^i > B^{(M-1:M)})}{1 - \delta_i(1 - \Pr(B^i > B^{(M-1:M)}))}
\tag{27}
$$

In this case if δ_i is known it is straight forward to determine $O^i(B_i)$. Let $H_2(.)$ denote the distribution of $B^{(M-1:M)}$ (the price), which is observed. Given this we can rewrite the option value as a function of observed variables.[20]

$$
O^i(B^i) = \frac{\delta_i H_2(B^i) \int_{\underline{b}}^{B^i} (B^i - B^{(M-1:M)}) h_2(B^{(M-1:M)}) dB^{(M-1:M)}}{(1 - \delta_i(1 - H_2(B^i)))}
\tag{28}
$$

It is often argued that real people cannot do the types of calculations that economists assume of them. In this case, eBay or some other service could provide a web based option calculator to calculate the bidder's option value and thus their optimal bid.[21] The following proposition gives the main result of the section.

---

[20]See Jofre-Bonet and Pesendorfer (2003) for a similar argument.

[21]I note that traders use such calculators in pricing options via the Black-Scholes formula, and that computer scientists are working on developing similar types of calculators for bidding in on-line auctions.

Proposition 8 *If Assumptions (1 - 4) and Assumptions (20 - 23), $H(.)$ is identified, $H_2(.)$ is observed and δ_i is known, then $F(.)$ is identified and $F(V^i) = F(B^i + O^i(B^i)) = H(B^i)$, where $O^i(B^i)$ is defined by Equation (28).*

Proof From Lemma 1 we have that $B_t^i = V^i - O^i(B^i)$ or $V^i = B^i + O^i(B^i)$. From Equation (28) $O(B^i)$ is a function of B^i, $H_2(.)$ and δ_i. Q.E.D.

The proposition states that if δ_i is known and stationary then it is straightforward to determine V^i from the observation of B^i and the observed distribution of prices $(H_2(.))$. Each bidder discounts her bid by her option value. If her discount factor is known, her option value can be calculated given her proposed bid (B^i), her discount factor (δ_i) and the distribution of prices (H_2). The problem of course is that in general δ_i is not observed.[22]

Assumption 24 *Let $\delta_i = \delta = 1 + r$*

Corollary 4 *If Assumptions (1 - 4) and Assumptions 20 - 23 and Assumption 24 hold, $H(.)$ is identified, $H_2(.)$ is observed and r is constant and observed, then $F(.)$ is identified and $F(V) = F(B + O(B)) = H(B)$.*

Proof. By Assumption 24, $\delta_i = 1 + r$, as r is observed, we have the result from Proposition 8. Q.E.D.

Corollary 4 states that if the interest rate (r) is known and it is assumed that every bidder's discount factor is exactly equal to $1 + r$, then the value distribution is identified. This result comes straight from Proposition 8 as the discount rate is known. If we assume that capital markets are perfect and each bidder is optimizing on an interior solution with respect to their choices over borrowing and saving, then it would be reasonable for the interest rate to determine every bidder's discount factor. The following result shows that if we have more information then it is possible for the value function to be

---

[22]See Rust (1994) for a discussion of the problem of identifying the decision maker's time preference in a dynamic decision making problem under uncertainty.

identified under less restrictive assumptions on each bidder's time preferences. In particular, if there is variation in the interest rates it is possible to identify time preferences that are an approximation around the interest rate. The following example shows that if interest rates follow simple Markov process with two mass points, it is possible to identify preferences up to a linear approximation.

Assumption 25 *Let r be distributed by a Markov process such that $\Pr(r_{t+1} = r_1 | r_t = r_2) = \Pr(r_{t+1} = r_2 | r_t = r_1) = q$ where $q \in (0, 1)$*

Assumption 26 *Let $\delta_i = 1 + r + \beta(1 + r)$.*

Assumption 26 states that each bidder's time preferences is a linear approximation around the interest rate. The following corollary states that given the variation in the interest rates and the time preferences of the bidders it is possible to identify both the value distribution $(F(.))$ and the time preference parameter (β).

Corollary 5 *If Assumptions (1 - 4) and Assumptions (20 - 23) and Assumption 25 and 26 hold, $H_{r_1}(B(r_1))$ and $H_{r_2}(B(r_2))$ are identified and H_{2r_1} and H_{2r_2} are observed, then $F(.)$ and β are identified, and $F(V) = F(B(r_1) + O(B(r_1)) = H_{r_1}(B(r_1))$ where $O(B(r_1))$ is defined below.*

Proof. Given the distribution of r we can write option value in a recursive fashion.

$$
\begin{aligned}
O(B(r_1)) &= (1 + r_1 + (1 + r_1)\beta) \\
&\quad \times (q(H_{r_1}(B(r_1))E(B(r_1) - B^{(M-1:M)}|B(r_1) > B^{(M-1:M)}) \\
&\quad + (1 - H_{r_1}(B(r_1)))O(B(r_1))) \\
&\quad + (1 - q)(H_{r_2}(B(r_2))E(B(r_2) - B^{(M-1:M)}|B(r_2) > B^{(M-1:M)}) \\
&\quad + (1 - H_{r_2}(B(r_2)))O(B(r_2))))
\end{aligned}
\tag{29}
$$

Similarly for $O(B(r_2))$. We have

$$
E(B(r_1)) - E(B(r_2)) = O(B(r_1)) - O(B(r_2))
\tag{30}
$$

28

Noting that the LHS is observed. It is tedious but straight forward to solve for β as a function of observables from $O(B(r_1))$, $O(B(r_2))$ and Equation (30). Q.E.D.

Corollary 5 states if the interest rate follows a simple Markov process and the distribution is known and observed by the bidders, then the value distribution can be identified when every bidder's discount factor is a simple linear function of the interest rate. The variation in bids caused by the changing interest rates can be used to identify the representative bidder's time preferences. It seems reasonable to expect that the more interest rate regimes there are, the more flexible the time preference function that can be identified.

The corollary shows that the richer the data the more flexible the assumptions on the approximation of the bidder's preferences over time. One useful feature of eBay data is that particular bidders can be tracked over time (see Arora et al. (2002) for an example of how this data can be used). If there is data on bidder characteristics such as their zip code or their reputation score, then it may be possible to use similar methods to identify demand when time preferences vary across observable characteristics of the bidder.

4.2 Differentiated Products

This section considers a bidder facing an infinite sequence of auctions for a single item, where the items offered in each auction are differentiated. In this case, Zeithammer (2004a) points out that knowledge of specific future auction affects bidding behavior. In particular, if a bidder learns that her preferred item will be sold in the next auction she may not bid in the current auction as the continuation payoff may be higher than the expected payoff of winning the current auction.

Consider the following model. The following assumption states that the bidder faces a sequence of auctions with two items ($\{C, D\}$) available in the sequence. Let V_c^i denote the bidders value for item C where V_c^i is distributed $F_c(.)$ and similarly for item D. Note that only item is available at a time and the bidder will leave the sequence once she wins an auction. For example if the items are cars the bidder will leave the sequence once she wins a car, irrespective of whether it is car C or car D.

Assumptions 27 and 28 generalize the model presented in the previous section.

Assumption 27 *Let each bidder i face a sequence of auctions $\mathcal{A}_t^i = \{A_t^{ij_t}, A_{t+1}^{ij_{t+1}}, ...\}$ where $i \in \mathcal{I}$ and item $j_t \in \{C, D\}$.*

Assumption 28 *The* ex ante *probability that the item in any auction A_t is C is p_c, with $p_d = 1 - p_c$.*

Assumption 29 states that the bidder may learn about the item to be auctioned in the next auction at any time during the current auction. The probability that she learns of the item's type at time s is denoted $q(s)$.

Assumption 29 *In each auction A_t, the probability the item type in auction A_{t+1} is revealed prior to $s \in [0, \tau]$ is $q(s)$, such that $q(\tau) \leq 1$.*

Lemma 2 *If Assumptions 21 and 22 and Assumptions 27, 28 and 29 hold, $V_c^i \neq V_d^i$ and the bidder's discount rate is close enough to 1, then in every Bayes Nash equilibrium, each bidder bids her value in each auction either after the item in the next auction is revealed or at her last opportunity, if she is not censored.*

A well known result in decision making under uncertainty is that if future information may affect the decision maker's optimal choice then in expectation the decision maker is strictly better off waiting for that information to be revealed before making the choice (Mirman et al. (1993)). In this case new information affects the option value of winning the current auction and thus the optimal bid. As discussed above there is preponderance for eBay bidders to have their high bids bunched towards the end of the auction. This result suggests that one explanation is that bidders are waiting for information about the items that will be available in future auctions.[23]

---

[23]See Roth and Ockenfels (2002) and Bajari and Hortacsu (2003) for a discussion of other explanations.

	CU	CC	CD	DU	DC	DD
CU	$p_c(1-q(t^i))$	$q(t^i)p_c^2$	$p_cq(t^i)p_d$	$p_d(1-q(t^i))$	$p_dq(t^i)p_c$	$q(t^i)p_d^2$
CC	$(1-q(t^i))$	$q(t^i)p_c$	$q(t^i)p_d$	0	0	0
CD	0	0	0	$(1-q(t^i))$	$q(t^i)p_c$	$q(t^i)p_d$
DU	$p_c(1-q(t^i))$	$q(t^i)p_c^2$	$p_cq(t^i)p_d$	$p_d(1-q(t^i))$	$p_dq(t^i)p_c$	$q(t^i)p_d^2$
DC	$(1-q(t^i))$	$q(t^i)p_c$	$q(t^i)p_d$	0	0	0
DD	0	0	0	$(1-q(t^i))$	$q(t^i)p_c$	$q(t^i)p_d$

Table 3: Transition probabilities

Given this result the bidder's problem has six states with the transition probabilities given in Table 3. The six states are CU which denotes that the bidders is currently in an auction for item C and the item in the next auction *unknown* (the bidder has not yet observed a signal). Similarly CC denotes a current auction for item C and it is known that the next auction is an auction for item C. The transition probabilities are determined by the *ex ante* probability that the item will be C (p_c) and the probability that the bidder observes a signal of the item to be auction off in the next auction prior to her "last opportunity" ($q(t^i)$). We can write down the bidder's option value of winning a particular auction in the following recursive manner.

$$
\begin{aligned}
O^i(B_{CU}^i) &= \delta_i(\textstyle\sum_K p_k H_k(B_k^i)E(B_k^i - B^{(M-1:M)}|B_k^i > B^{(M-1:M)}) \\
&+ (1 - H_k(B_k^i))O^i(B_k^i))
\end{aligned}
\tag{31}
$$

where $K = \{CU, CC, CD, DU, DC, DD\}$, p_k denotes the transition probability described above, and $H_k(.)$ is the distribution of bids conditional on the state. The following proposition states that given certain assumptions we can identify the underlying conditional value functions from data generated by bidders facing such a decision making problem.

Proposition 9 *If Assumptions 21, 22 and 24 and Assumptions 27, 28 and 29 hold, $H_k(.)$ is identified and H_{2k} is observed for all $k \in K$, then $F_j(.)$ is identified for each $j \in \{C, D\}$ and $F_C(V) = F_C(B_{CU}+O(B_{CU})) = H_{CU}(B_{CU})$ and similarly for $F_D(.)$.*

31

Proof. Given Lemma 2 and the discussion presented above, the proof is similar to the proof of Corollary 5. Q.E.D.

As long as it is possible to observe the distribution of prices conditional on the six states of the world, we can identify the underlying value function for each state (using methods described in Song (2003) and in the previous sections). Once we have these and we know the time preference of the bidders it is just a matter of using the option value functions and some algebra to determine the underlying conditional value distributions.

5   Conclusion

There are three major issues with using eBay data to estimate the demand for an item. The first is that some bids and bidders are censored because potential bidders enter an auction after the price has risen above their willingness to pay. The second issue is that there may be observed and unobserved heterogeneity across bidders, items and auctions. The third issue is that an eBay bidder does not face a single auction for a single item, but rather faces a sequence of auctions for a single item. This paper looks at each issue in turn.

The first section develops on ideas presented in Song (2003) and Athey and Haile (2002), and suggests an alternative method for identifying demand in single eBay auctions. Athey and Haile (2002) shows that in certain auctions demand can be identified from observing the price and the number of bidders. Unfortunately, in general eBay auctions it is not possible to observe the number of bidders. Song (2003) shows that for a certain set of eBay auctions it is possible to identify demand even when the number of bidders is unknown if the distribution of *two* order statistics are observed. However, in many cases it is not possible to observe two order statistics in eBay auctions. This paper presents two alternative approaches. The first assumes a particular distribution on the number of potential bidders. The second makes an additional structural assumption. It is shown that under these additional assumptions, the distribution of values is identified.

The second section generalizes the results of the first section to the case where there is auction heterogeneity. The paper shows that a traditional demand model is non-parametrically identified using eBay type data. The model allows for general functional form relationships between observable characteristics of the item and the bidder and unobserved item heterogeniety. The proof of the proposition suggests a method for non-parametrically estimating the model. Athey and Haile (2002) show that when the number of bidders is known the underlying value distribution can be identified when there is unobserved auction heterogeneity. The section presents assumptions and requirements on the data for identification in this case where the number of bidders is unknown.

The third section considers an eBay bidder facing an infinite sequence of auctions for a single item. Following Dixit and Pindyck (1994), Zeithammer (2004a,b), Arora et al. (2002) and others, it is shown that winning an eBay auction can be thought of as "killing" an option to bid on a future auction for the same item. The implication is that the value of the item won is equal to its actual value less the value of the item's option. We can thus reinterpret the value of the item in a single auction in this way. Following Song (2003) it is still a BNE for all bidders to bid their value for the item in each auction (if they have the opportunity to bid at their last opportunity). Thus the distribution of values for the item in a particular auction is identified following Song (2003) and the results in the first section. The section shows that given certain data requirements and certain assumptions on each bidder's preferences over time, the value distribution for the item that is independent of any particular auction can be identified.

References

Adams, Christopher P. and Laura Bivins, "Demand for Cars on eBay," January 2004. Federal Trade Commission.

_ , **William Vogt, and Hao Xu**, "Digital Demand: The demand for digital cameras on eBay," March 2004. Federal Trade Commission.

Arora, Ashish, Hao Xu, Rema Padman, and William Vogt, "Optimal Bidding in Sequential Online Auctions," 2002. Heinz School of Public Policy, Carnegie Mellon University.

Athey, Susan and Philip Haile, "Identification in Standard Auction Models," *Econometrica*, 2002, *70* (6), 2170–2140.

Bajari, Patrick and Ali Hortacsu, "Winner's Curse, Reserve Prices, and Endogenous Entry: Empirical Insights from eBay Auctions," *RAND Journal of Economics*, 2003, *34* (2).

_ **and** _ , "Economic Insights from Internet Auctions," February 2004. Duke University.

_ **and C. Lanier Bankard**, "Demand Estimation with Heterogenous Consumer and Unobserved Product Characteristics: A Hedonic Approach," January 2004. Stanford University.

Berry, Steven, James Levinsohn, and Ariel Pakes, "Automobile Prices in Market Equilibrium," *Econometrica*, 1995, *60* (4), 889–917.

Cohen, Adam, *The Perfect Store: Inside eBay*, first ed., Little, Brown and Company, 2002.

Deltas, George, "Auction Size and Price Dynamics in Sequential Auctions," February 1999. University of Illinois.

Dixit, Avinash K. and Robert S. Pindyck, *Investment Under Uncertainty*, Princeton University Press, 1994.

Froeb, Luke, Steven Tschantz, and Philip Crooke, "Second-Price Auctions with Power-Related Distributions," February 2001. Vanderbilt University.

Greene, William, *Econometric Analysis*, fourth ed., Prentice Hall, 2000.

Guerre, E, I Perrigne, and Q Vuong, "Optimal Nonparametric Estimation of First-Price Auctions," *Econometrica*, 2000, *68*, 525–574.

Jofre-Bonet, Mireia and Martin Pesendorfer, "Estimation of a Dynamic Auction Game," *Econometrica*, September 2003, *71* (5), 1443–1489.

Krasnokutskaya, Elena, "Identification and Estimation in Highway Procurement Auctions under Unobserved Auction Heterogeniety," August 2003. University of Pennsylvania.

Lucking-Reiley, David, "Auctions on the Internet: What's Being Auctioned and How?," *The Journal of Industrial Economics*, September 2000, *68* (3), 227–252.

Mirman, Leonard, Larry Samuelson, and Amparo Urbano, "Monopoly Experimentation," *International Economic Review*, 1993, *34* (3), 549–563.

Nevo, Aviv, "A Practicioner's Guide to Estimation of Random-Coefficients Logit Models of Demand," *Journal of Economics and Management Strategy*, 2000, *9* (4), 513–548.

Resnick, Paul, Richard Zeckhauser, John Swanson, and Kate Lockwood, "The Value of Reputation on EBay: A controlled experiment," May 2003. University of Michigan.

Rezende, Leonardo, "Auction Econometrics by Least Squares," November 2002. University of Illinois.

Roth, Alvin E. and Axel Ockenfels, "Last-Minute Bidding and the Rules for Ending Second-Price Auctions: Evidence from eBay and Amazon Auctions on the Internet," *American Economic Review*, September 2002, *92* (4), 1093–1103.

Rust, John, *Structural Estimation of Markov Decision Processes*, Vol. 4 of *Handbook of Econometrics*, Amsterdam: North-Holland, R.F. Engel and D.L. McFadden (eds).

Song, Unjy, "Nonparametric Estimation of an eBay Auction Model with an Unknown Number of Bidders," November 2003. University of Wisconsin.

Zeithammer, Robert, "Forward-looking Bidders in Sequential Auctions: A Theory of Bargain-hunting on eBay," September 2003. University of Chicago.

_ , "Forward-Looking Bidding in Online Auctions," April 2004. University of Chicago.

_ , "A Theory of Sequential Auctions with Information about Future Goods," April 2004. University of Chicago.

Zhang, Alex, Dirk Beyer, Julie Ward, Tongwei Liu, Alan Karp, Kemal Guler, Shailendra Jain, and Hsiu-Khuern Tang, "Modeling the Price-Demand Relationship Using Auction Bid Data," July 2002. Hewlett-Packard.